HALLE WEENIE

Author: Amiee Entwistle
Illustrator: Sirisha Nandalur

To my loving husband Eliot and my sweet son Eliot Jr.
Thank you for your love and support.
You make my life wonderful.
Love, Amiee

◆

For my Kiran
For my three sweet little witches, Reyna, Avani and Karina
For my Neema
For all those who fight with all their might, think they can't, but do anyway
Love, Sirisha

Designed by: Vince Pannullo
Illustrator: Sirisha Nandalur
Printed in the United States of America by RJ Communications.
ISBN: 978-0-578-14990-5

Dear Parents,

Do you often wonder what to do with all the extra Halloween candy your children receive each year? Every October we have an abundance of candy at our house. Between the left over candy from Easter to all of the fun fall events we attend, one little boy could not possibly eat the amount of candy we accumulate. Of course we all love the chocolate, caramel, and yummy sugar sweets, but we also know how unhealthy it is to have an overload of candy in our diets.

I wrote the book Halle Weenie after starting a new tradition in our family. My son, Eliot, an only child, was four years old when the magic began for him. I explained to him I had heard of a cute little witch named Halle that needed some candy to make her teeth icky. She wanted to be like the other witches that had brown, black and green teeth. Because her teeth were sparkling white, she needed some extra sugar to make her as scary as the other witches. I also explained to Eliot that if he left her some candy on the front porch at nighttime Halle would leave him a present. That was all he needed to hear! It wasn't even his birthday or Christmas, and he was going to get a present! We sat on the floor and separated candy for Eliot and candy for the witch. Halle came to our house that night and left him Spiderman socks and a Spiderman hat. He was so excited to get a present that he wanted to give Halle more candy!

After that fun experience I decided to share Halle with my friends and family. Now I would like to share Halle with you and your children. Halle doesn't leave expensive and over-the-top gifts. She just wants to say thanks for sharing by giving something small and memorable.

Many local dental offices and churches accept extra candy and send the donations to the troops overseas or to people in need. I hope your family enjoys the Halle Weenie tradition as much as we do. Don't forget to brush twice a day!

Blessings to you and your family,

Amiee Entwistle

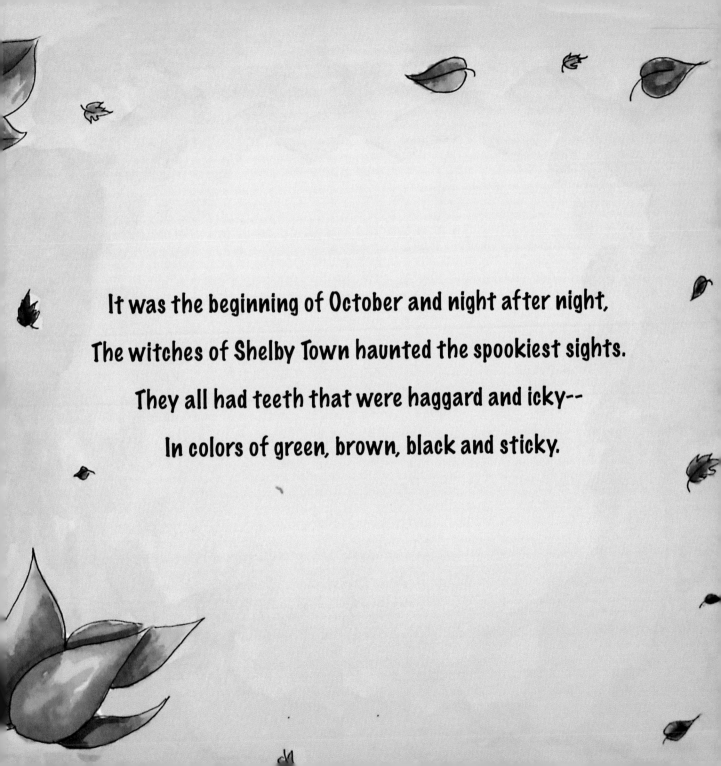

It was the beginning of October and night after night,

The witches of Shelby Town haunted the spookiest sights.

They all had teeth that were haggard and icky--

In colors of green, brown, black and sticky.

They wanted to scare kids with frightening looks--

Wickedly laughing as children shivered and shook.

The witch Halle Weenie had a smile so white.

Eating apples and oranges made her teeth bright.

She wanted her mouth to look creepy and chilling--

But knew what she ate would not lead to fillings.

Her glimmering sparkles made Halle so mad.

It caused her to do something terribly bad.

She went out at dusk for her nightly broom ride,

And noticed some sweets in a window opened wide.

Night after night she snuck from the dish.

Her teeth turned green, just as she wished.

The yummy treats began to disappear,

And Halle saw Eliot count his candy with tears.

"I had caramel and cocoa in this sugary mix!"

The boy Eliot cried seeking a chocolate fix.

Halle had to admit what she did wasn't right.

She decided to leave him a surprise that night.

Attaching it to the gift, she left him a note.

It started with, "Dear Eliot", and here's what she wrote:

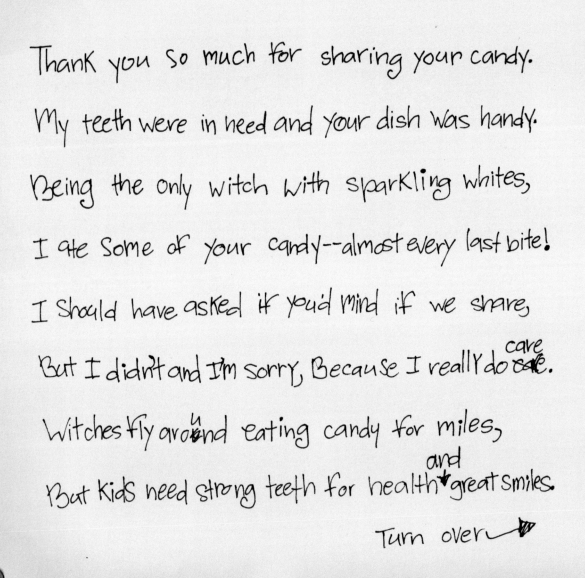

Thank you so much for sharing your candy.

My teeth were in need and your dish was handy.

Being the only witch with sparkling whites,

I ate some of your candy--almost every last bite!

I should have asked if you'd mind if we share,

But I didn't and I'm sorry, Because I really do ~~care~~ care.

Witches fly around eating candy for miles,

But kids need strong teeth for health and great smiles.

Turn over

I want you to know sweets damage your spikes.

Eat more fruits and veggies, which every kid likes.

I'm leaving a gift to say you're great!

This is to repay you for the candy I ate.

I hope we're okay, and you don't think I'm a meanie

♥ Love,

The sweet tooth witch,

Halle Weenie

The next day awaking to find the surprise,

Eliot read the letter with tears in his eyes.

Grabbing the note and gift, he would tell,

His buddies the news to make their teeth well.

"Children need teeth, as they help us to eat!
Let's not lose them like witches; we'll have healthier treats!
Give Halle the witch your extra Halloween candy.
You won't be sorry; she'll leave you something handy."

And that's how it started,
a story so sweet.
Set out your extra
trick-or-treats!